Revised and Updated Edition

© 2008 - 2021

All rights reserved. Printed in the United States of America. No part of this book may be used or reproduced in any manner whatsoever, stored in a retrieval system or transmitted by any means electronic, mechanical, photocopied, recorded or otherwise, without written permission of the publisher.

For more information about the book and professional development training, contact Caroline Brewer, Unchained Spirit Enterprises, at caroline.brewer@carolinebrewerbooks.com or visit:
www.carolinebrewerbooks.com

Table of Contents

FAQ 3

What Educators & Advocates Are Saying 7

What is the Happy Teacher Strategy? 8

A Deliberate System 10

Relationships 11

HTHS Phrases to Build Good Relationships 12

Reading 14

Why I Read 15

Reading: How to Get Students Interested 17

Rhyme 19

Rhythm 21

Repetition 24

Rap 27

Routines 30

Release and Relax 35

The Rapture, Eye Scissors 38

Walks, Fountains & Peace Gardens 39

Relevance 41

Recreation 45

Background 48

Creating Vocabulary "BINGO" Cards 50

Vocabulary "BINGO" Card 51

60 Sets of "BINGO" Rhyming Words 52

48 Vocabulary "BINGO" Words 53

Bibliography 54

About the Authors 56

FAQ

What is the Happy Teacher/Happy Students strategy?

The Happy Teacher/Happy Students (HTHS) strategy is a deliberate, holistic, and joyful system of intrinsic motivation for effectively educating children.

The Happy Teacher/Happy Students strategy meets the NCATE (National Council for the Accreditation of Teacher Education) Approved Curriculum Guidelines of the ACEI (Association for Childhood Education International) for the basic preparation of elementary education teachers, and does wonders for the education of middle and high school students.

What prompted the creation of the Happy Teacher/Happy Students strategy?

Teachers and children prompted the creation of the HTHS strategy. Every interaction. The questions, the answers, the praise, the criticism, the analysis, the tears, the anger, the excitement, the hunger to learn and teach with joy, and more than anything, the progress, the transformations, the magic. This manual is full of their stories.

And then, in 2006, I met Joshua Smith, not long after I began using the Happy Teacher/Happy Students strategies with D.C. public schools students and he asked me the secret to the success. I didn't have a ready answer, so he urged me to find and document it. I began to review the strategies I'd used and then write explanations for them. Joshua provided additional research based on his expertise in mind, movement, and behavior therapies. The strategy is laid out using 11 words that begin with the letter R: Relationships, Reading, Rhythm, Rhyme, Repetition, Rap, Routines, Release and Relax, Relevance, and Recreation. You'll learn more in the following pages.

I wrote this training manual and a book of philosophy about the Happy Teacher/Happy Students in the summer of 2006, but before publishing them wanted to do more research. In addition to uncovering empirical research about some of the best-known approaches, I found books and movies about some of America's most effective teachers. I studied what made them successful and discovered that they all used most, if not all, of the 11 Rs, but without identifying their approaches in those terms.

Finally, my dear friend and former Veteran Teacher Marni Barron, became the first teacher in the world to use the HTHS strategy daily and with such a powerful effect that I became thoroughly convinced of its power to revolutionize teaching and learning. I will be forever grateful to her for trusting me and this work.

FAQ

Which R is the most important, the foundation?

Relationships is the most important R. It's the foundation for every other strategy. Every effective teacher has excellent relationships with their students. It doesn't mean they do everything perfectly or never have bad days. It just means the health of the relationship is the lens through which we operate. The late longtime Educator Clare Cherry shared great advice about how to keep the teacher-student relationship healthy when she said, "What I want for myself, I must also want for you. What I want from you, I must also be willing to give."

Also, Professor Carol Manigault has pointed out that researchers long ago concluded that, in an overwhelmingly negative atmosphere, filled with negative expectations, it is impossible for students to perform as well as when they are treasured and considered worthwhile and valued.

The definition of a child is an immature being. Children are by nature immature. We must accept that and be okay with it because it's the truth, and this truth gives us all room to grow and develop. At the same time, we must know that we can't succeed without having strong, healthy, positive relationships with children.

That said, I love all the Rs. In fact, I created a song to help teachers remember them so that they'll easily come to mind when building lesson plans and delivering instruction. Many of the Rs are tightly interwoven. For instance, recreation and relevance are great relationship-builders. In fact, it's very difficult to have a good relationship with students if we don't incorporate fun into our approach to teaching. And if the lessons aren't relevant to what students experience in their daily lives, we will find it harder, if not impossible, to connect with them.

How would the Happy Teacher/Happy Students work with the national education reform model? (Response from Marni Barron, former teacher, DCPS)

"I'd like to think HTHS was made for this moment in education, as confusing and controversial and challenging as it is. One plus of the current reform model is that it stresses well-organized and objective-driven lesson planning and delivery. The HTHS approach provides strategies to release the tension and pressure that such a model might create while providing opportunities for students and teachers to enjoy the teaching and learning experience. We all learn and perform at higher rates when we enjoy the experience.

The Happy Teacher/Happy Students strategy is also results-driven. When teachers and children see quickly that they are succeeding at new levels, they are motivated to continue working toward even larger goals. The strategies are based on love and supportive measures. Research has shown that these approaches work best for both child and adult."

FAQ

What is your analysis of other literacy and learning programs, such as Harvard's Earning by Learning Program? (Answered by Carol Manigault, Professor of Math and Computer Science at Felician University, NJ)

"Literacy is the foundation, the key, to all formal learning. The Happy Teacher/Happy Students is a gem of a system that trains teachers and awakens students in developing the LOVE to read and write as it builds proficiency in both. Rarely are those two objectives combined in an educational program. The goal of the HTHS is teaching children to read and write well and to love reading and writing, while valuing each student as a prized human being and *expecting* dramatic results to be realized.

According to the extensive research of Kenneth Bain, PhD, we should consider that there are basically three types of learners: 1) Surface Learners, 2) Strategic Learners – Students who figure out what they need to do to get an A, don't really want to know the material, but will learn enough to get a passing grade 3) Deep Learners – To learn deeply, you're curious and want to know something about what you're learning.

The key to what makes this work is the question the individual asks about the subject. In most classrooms, students are not the ones asking the questions. It's the teacher who tells them what to consider and how. Bain's work, known around the world, has investigated intrinsic as well as extrinsic motivation. Intrinsic motivation is the student asking questions, or being encouraged to use the right brain to think of new ways to view a subject. External motivation has to do with some kind of judgment or other influence being placed on your learning, such as grades or money.

Bain was able to show that when the concept of grades was introduced shortly after the industrial revolution, student motivation to learn changed. Students no longer learned for the sake of learning. They learned with an eye toward what grade or reward they would get for what they could demonstrate they learned. His work has proven that extrinsic motivation never generates a love of learning. The Happy Teacher/Happy Students strategy is on a mission to inspire a love of learning."

FAQ

What does the Happy Teacher/Happy Students strategy look like in a classroom?

It looks like a social-emotional and intellectual revolution, where:

The boy who never smiled would start smiling
And the girl who never wrote would start writing
And the boy who never read would start reading

And the boy who always cursed would stop cursing
And the girl who liked to fight would stop fighting
And the boy who talked too much would stop talking – too much

And the girl who used to hide would stop hiding
And the boy who used to lie would stop lying
And the girl who hated words would start liking them (and loving you)

And the girl who always said no would start saying yes
And the boy who couldn't write a complete sentence would write complete sentences
And the boy who wasn't in your class would come to your class
because of the *buzz* about your class

And the boy who barely knew the alphabet would learn to read well enough to ace tests

And the girl who was always angry would become mostly happy
And the boy who was depressed would start (moon) walking on sunshine
And the girl who was always mad would find peace with the world

And the boy who didn't believe in himself would express faith in himself
And the girl who was always feisty would show her vulnerable side (and thank you)
And the boy who didn't like to read would love listening to himself - read

And the girl who was always scared would no longer be afraid
And the boy who was at the bottom academically would rise to the top
And the girl who never moved would one day rise from her chair and dance to the music only she could hear (and all of her peers would clap for her)

And all of these marvelous things with children would happen
because you had the courage to say yes when everyone else was saying no,
to express faith when everyone else had stopped believing,
to think about what could be when everyone else was thinking about what had been, because you have watched from afar the start of many revolutions
and now you know you can't rest...until you start your own.

What Educators & Advocates Are Saying

"The Happy Teacher is a must for all educators intent on improving instruction, reaching the seemingly disconnected student, and creating magic within the classroom."
– *Cheryl Thomas, Veteran English Teacher and Ed.D., Educational Leadership, Northeast Indiana*

"Two days after the training, we had the worst day in our school. The kids in my last period were acting up in all their other classes. But by the time our class was over, Ms. Brewer and the Happy Teacher strategies had made a believer out of me. For the first time, every student in class participated in our reading lesson. One student, who has every learning disability diagnosis imaginable and is on medication, not only participated in class, but went ahead to read the book I assigned. Another student who was the worst behaved in our school started participating after I spoke to him using the Happy Teacher phrases to stop bad behavior. He had another great day the next day and came back to class, hugged and thanked me. The Happy Teacher training saved my teaching life."
– *LaQuisha Hall, 18-year teacher, Baltimore, MD*

"The most important strategy I wanted to learn was ways to engage students, and I learned that. After returning to my classroom, I realized that when I go back to my old ways, out of habit, I get limited results with my students. When I remember to say the phrases I learned in the training, such as, 'I need you...,' I have gotten the desired response. I recommend the Happy Teacher training because of the helpful tools I have received to be even more effective."
– *Lauren Tate, Presidential Excellence Award Winner 2011, Peabody Elementary School, Washington, D.C.*

"Literacy is the foundation, the key, to all formal learning. The Happy Teacher is a gem of a system that trains teachers and awakens students in developing the *love* to read and write as it builds proficiency in both. Rarely are those two objectives combined in an educational program."
– *Carol Manigault, Professor of Math and Computer Science at Felician College, New Jersey*

What is the Happy Teacher Strategy?

The Happy Teacher/Happy Students strategy is a holistic professional development and educational approach that balances cognitive and non-cognitive (emotional) instruction to create healthy and joyous teaching and learning experiences.

The Happy Teacher/Happy Students strategy can be used as a complement and supplement to other reading programs, or as a set of strategies to tackle literacy, other academic subjects, intellectual and social-emotional growth and development and learning deficits head-on.

The Happy Teacher/Happy Students strategy allows schools and districts to build capacity and provides long-term sustainability at a comparatively low cost.

Its approaches and companion children's books help educators and childcare providers more effectively meet state and federal learning standards.

It inspires success across the curricula.

Companion books contain social and emotional content that engages and meets the needs of hungry readers (students who are hungry to improve as readers).

Using elements such as movement, dance, art, shorter intervals of instruction, frequent recreation breaks, the release of tension through vocalizations, games, relaxation techniques, repetition, classroom and behavior management routines, rhymes, storytelling, and enhanced teacher communication through empathy and breathing, the HTHS has successfully demonstrated the strategies that help children perform better academically.

In short, students absorb information more quickly and completely and retain it longer when they have the tools and the permission to safely and productively discharge emotional stress, participate in learning, and express themselves with confidence.

What is the Happy Teacher Strategy?

The Happy Teacher/Happy Students strategy meets the NCATE (National Council for the Accreditation of Teacher Education) Approved Curriculum Guidelines of the ACEI (Association for Childhood Education International) for the basic preparation of elementary education teachers, which include standards such as:

Reading, writing, and oral language integration.

Opportunities for speaking and writing that vary in form, tone, subject, purpose, audience, point of view, and style.

Ways to promote reading and oral language development for personal growth, lifelong learning, enjoyment, and insight into the human experience.

Inclusion of the literature of childhood, including knowing a range of books, how to share them with students, and how to guide students to respond in a variety of ways.

Promoting creative thinking and expression, as through storytelling, drama, choral and oral reading, imaginative writing, and the like.

Recognizes the importance of *using reading in positive ways* in the classroom.

Recognizes the importance of creating *a supportive and positive environment for literacy learning.*

Give learners opportunities in all aspects of literacy as readers, authors, and thinkers.

Recognizes the importance of implementing literacy programs designed *to meet the needs of readers* rather than imposing prescribed and inflexible programs.

Uses text to stimulate interest in promoting interest in reading growth, fostering appreciation for the written word, and increasing the motivation of learners to read widely and independently for information and pleasure.

Models and discusses reading as a valuable activity.

Engages students in activities that develop their image of themselves as literate.

Provides regular opportunities for learners to select from a wide variety of books/quality written materials. Provides opportunities for students to be exposed to various purposes for reading and writing, to experience reading and writing as relevant to themselves, to write and have their writing responded to in a positive way.

A Deliberate System

Most importantly, what you will find within the **Happy Teacher/Happy Students** is a <u>Deliberate System</u>.

Psychology Professor Anders Ericsson of Florida State University offers this take on Deliberate Systems. "Whatever innate differences two people may exhibit in their abilities to memorize, those differences are swamped by how well each person 'encodes' the information." The best way to learn how to encode information meaningfully is through a process known as "*deliberate practice*," or a deliberate system.

So here you have scientific research that emphasizes that *the way* a person encodes information is key to *how well they will remember* that information and are able to use it to succeed.

Deliberate practice works because it addresses how the brain adapts thought to action. Success is a matter of repetition, guidance, and goal-setting. Examples of deliberate practice, technique, and feedback are throughout this book. In the African tradition of stretching memory to its outer limits, I offer you a "deliberate practice" for memorizing the 11 Rs.

The 11 Rs Song by Caroline Brewer ©2006

Reading, Rhythm and **Rhyyyme…**

Make Sure You Keep Good Tiiime…

Rap, Repetition and **Relevance** (sing quickly)

Give Children A Chance to see It Make Sense

Release and **Relax** in Your **Rooou-tines.**

Include **Recreation** in Everything!

(Take a deep breath, exhale!)

And Don't Forget (repeat this line and each that follows it once)

Your **Relationships**

With the Chil-dren!

*Sing the song at least five times in a row – taking a deep breath after each time through and breathing as much as you can throughout the song. After 30 minutes of doing another activity, see if you can recall all 11 Rs by singing the song. If not, go back, sing it five more times, take a break and repeat until you know it by heart. Enjoy!

Happy Teacher and Happy Students Training Manual   Caroline Brewer

Relationships

It is so important to understand and remind ourselves regularly of why we teach. The book I wrote, *Why I Teach* provides excellent opportunities to reflect and motivate ourselves during the school year.

When we understand why we teach, it's easier to focus on maintaining a good relationship with each child. When we understand why we teach, we should have no trouble observing longtime teacher Clare Cherry's Golden Rule of Awareness: *"What I want for myself, I must also want for you; what I want from you I must also be willing to give."*

It would become clear that, as she points out, *"Children usually live up to and perform according to our expectations."* Therefore, it is essential that we establish with our students respectful relationships with high expectations.

Steve R. Covey, *Author of 7 Habits of Highly Effective People*, says adopting a philosophy of Win-Win, "It's not your way or my way, but a better way, a higher way" leads to successful relationships. "You basically get what you reward," he says, so we should reward what we want – behavior that's at the highest level.

Seeing children as we want them to be instead of how they might be acting is key to building and maintaining good relationships. Seeing and engaging with children in a higher and more positive light is a way to practice high expectations and help them embrace their true identities and potential as lifelong learners.

Education Guru Harry Wong, who lists high expectations as one of three keys to effective teaching, recommends a promise, similar to the one below, to establish good relationships and maintain high expectations. It's also Win-Win.

The PROMISE

Dear Students: You are going to have a great time learning in my class. **I PROMISE.**

I am a professional. I've been an author (insert your profession and details) for many years. I have written a dozen books and hosted hundreds of seminars on this topic. I love what I do and with my expertise and experiences, I can help you go further than you ever imagined.

But, I need an orderly environment for that to happen. I need you to follow the rules and procedures that we establish. I need you to treat your classmates kindly and fairly. I need you to work with one another as team members. I need you to participate, ask questions, and be honest with me when things are troubling you. I promise you will succeed. ***But I need your help.***

If I told you that I could make you a millionaire, would you trust me to help you become one too? Well, I might not be able to help you make millions. What I *can* do is give you a great experience in this classroom that will make you *feel* like a millionaire. I can help you learn to read and write well and enjoy it. These skills will greatly expand the choices you have to live the kind of life you desire. We will succeed. With your help. **I PROMISE.**

Happy Teacher and Happy Students Training Manual   *Caroline Brewer*

HTHS Phrases to Build Good Relationships

How can I help you?

How can I help you have
a great day?

How do you feel?

I need your help.

Thank you
for your help.

I want you
to succeed.

I believe
in you.

I care about you.

There's so much good
in you.

You can do it. I'll help you.

Will you join us?

We would love for you to join us.

Thank you for joining us.

Relationships Notes

Reading

You may have tangible wealth untold;
Caskets of jewels and coffers of gold.
But richer than I you could never be.
I've got (somebody) who READS to me.

-(Slightly Revised) Strickland Gilliam

According to the National Center for Education Statistics (NCES), "Reading to young children promotes language acquisition and literacy development and, later on, achievement in reading comprehension and overall success in school."

Studies also show that it exposes children to a much wider and richer variety of texts than they could acquaint themselves with alone and it helps them understand the many purposes for acquiring good reading skills.

NCES has found that "the percentage of young children read aloud to daily by a family member is one indicator of how well young children are prepared for school. In particular, a mother's education is consistently related to whether or not children are read to by a family member."

One study cited by a web site dedicated to Dr. Seuss found that there is only one book per child in the homes of every 300 low-income children. Middle-income homes average 13 books per child. Reading Guru Jim Trelease reports that most low-income homes have more TV sets than books.

These facts inform us that most low-income children and many middle income children are not receiving the reading stimulation and scaffolding from home that they need to reach their social, emotional, or intellectual potential.

Trelease, renowned author of *The Read Aloud Handbook*, has compiled numerous cases of parents who simply read aloud to their children every day and nurtured them into top students, including children labeled "dyslexic, mentally retarded, autistic," and with other disabilities. Reading aloud is the best college and life prep program in the world – and as long as we have libraries or people willing to share their books for free – the investment is only in time.

Teachers, interestingly, can make up a huge part of this gap with literacy immersion. One key to turning on children to the power of reading is to ask them why anyone should read. You'll be surprised and delighted at how they respond. Check out the poem for my answers and for an interactive (responsive reading) reading opportunity to launch your reading adventure.

Why I Read

by Caroline Brewer © 2005 (Excerpts)

Have fun reading this poem to your students responsively. Depending on reading level, the teacher can read the regular print as the students read the bold print. Or feel free to mix it up and have each student read one line in a performance roundtable.

I read because it's an adventurous thing.
I hug a book like it's a **DIAMOND RING**.
I read lyrics that make me want to **SING!**

Sometimes I read like **CRAZY**.
Can't call us readers **LAZY**.
I hurry up and read real **FAST,**
hopping from the bus to the train.
Sometimes, though, I read **SLOW,** to make the **STO-RY LAST**!

I get tickled by Seuss' ***GREEN EGGS AND HAM,***
and that pesky little character, you know, **SAM-I-AM!**
I read to answer questions that trouble my sleep.
Reading dissolves puzzles that run deep-sea deep.
I read with the excitement of summer and spring.
I read 'cause ain't nothing better I can do for this **BRAIN!**
I read with hope that for better
our world will soon **CHANGE!**
I read myself right into the magic of my lifelong **DREAMS!**

I read because it gives me information that I don't know.
I read Langston Hughes' **POETRY** 'cause the brother's got flow.

Why I Read

I read to find the **LIGHT!**
Sometimes it's out of **MY SIGHT!**
I read when it's **HARD!**
I got books by the **YARD!**

I read when it's silent,
Just me **BY MYSELF.**
I read, on accident, you know,
the signs on buses, trains, and buildings,
Just like **EVERYBODY ELSE!**

I will **NEVER** stop reading, No matter the struggle or strife.
See, my ancestors hardly got the chance.
So that's **INSPIRATION** for life.
Nobody will cut my ears if they see me with **A BOOK**,
Or slice my back with whips that bend me to shame.
Reading helps me shape **MY FUTURE** and boldly reclaim
our people's **PROUD** history. We are no longer in **CHAINS!**

So wipe your weeping eyes.
I read because **MAYA ANGELOU** told us, we've got reason to **RISE.**
I rise and I read because reading sets me free and **FREE** I plan to stay.
So if you don't like my reading, friend, **ADIOS,** and I wish you a **NICE DAY!**

Reading: How to Get Students Interested

During the Happy Teacher/Happy Students training, we explain that reading is related to snowflakes. We ask teachers/students to think about how nice it is to see a snowflake. Softly it falls from the sky to the ground and as you watch it dance, a twinkle appears in your eye and a little smile creases your face. But then, if the snow begins to fall faster and develops into a blizzard, your smile starts to turn into a little concern – especially if you're at school and didn't remember to bring your hat, mittens, or boots.

A few snowflakes here and there are not dangerous. But a blizzard – that's another story!

The same holds true with books. Having one book fall into our lives every now and then doesn't change anything. But if we get a blizzard of books into our lives, then it's going to make a huge difference. That's what we want children to have and read – a blizzard's worth of books.

Studies show that the more books a child reads and is exposed to the better reader he becomes.

One of the most effective ways to get children interested in and excited about reading is for teachers to read books, newspaper and magazine articles, comics, plays, and poetry to and with them – often. Research from organizations, such as the National Institute for Literacy, support this conclusion.

Jim Trelease, author of *The Read Aloud Handbook*, shared the results of a 1996 University of Southern California research study. The researchers examined the print climate in the classrooms of three California communities. They found that students in schools with book ratios of only three books to every one pupil (versus the national average of 18:1) had low reading scores. Few of those students went on to college.

Teachers must find time in the day – every day – to read to students. The Happy Teacher/Happy Students professional development training will show teachers a variety of fun and exciting ways to get reading into everyday instruction and to help children reach the conclusion that reading more and being read to are habits they want to embrace.

*Echo and Choral Reading, Call-and-Response, Responsive Reading, Dramatic Reading, Singing, Rapping, and Round-Robin Reading are interactive ways to get students excited about reading and boost their literacy skills.

Reading Notes

Rhyme

What do Jay-Z, Mother Goose, Queen Latifah and Dr. Seuss have in common? Most students can tell you. They are rhyme masters and have used this wonderful tool to become rich and/or famous. Mother Goose, of course, is just a composite character to whom hundreds of nursery rhymes are credited. Still, her collection of rhymes captivates us from infancy and holds sway until the grave. Nursery rhymes have been a category on the popular TV show *Jeopardy!* We never, ever forget those nursery rhymes. Nor do we forget the magical and innocent images of childhood that they engender.

This is why rhymes and rhyming books are excellent tools for helping emerging readers, of all ages, increase their skills instantly and for the long term.

Literacy experts tell us that rhymes build memory, vocabulary, and confidence *faster than any other reading technique*. Confidence is crucial in helping struggling readers see themselves as fluent, successful readers.

Read-Aloud Guru Jim Trelease advises, "Rhymes are the closest things to a mother's heartbeat. They are comfortable and predictable." No wonder children love them!

Rhymes, of course, are introduced to children at infancy and help them take their first steps up the rungs of literacy achievement. After listening to nursery rhymes during toddler and pre-school years, rhymes are key to the next huge step in language acquisition as children learn the alphabet.

Rhymes and songs make it easier for children to understand letter sounds, hear all the words, understand how words are put together, how to speak and read with emotion, how to be better writers and spellers, and how to recall words and ideas.

Importantly, rhymes are fun. When children enjoy reading and being read to, they are more likely to want to read on their own. Rhymes also are a highly effective way to teach difficult concepts across the curriculum. They provide educators with unlimited opportunities to boost a child's achievement level.

In 2006, I spoke to Raymond Mark, then high school math department chair at a school outside New York City. Raymond sings the quadratic formula to the tune of *Pop Goes The Weasel* and *Row, Row, Row Your Boat* to his Algebra II students. The formula is used to calculate such things as the precise timing of missiles and rocket launches. Having an easy way to remember the formula is a gift. Raymond's students absolutely love and are grateful for it! But many of his colleagues are too "embarrassed" to share the rhyming formula with their students. Imagine how many more students, especially in low-performing high schools, we could entice to take high-level math classes if they knew that complex formulas could be easily digested with rhyming schemes.

Remember nimble Jack? "Jack be nimble, Jack be quick, Jack jump over the candle-stick." Let's emulate Jack's skill in getting children over learning obstacles. Use rhymes to be nimble. Use rhymes to be quick. Rhymes boost reading and scholarly achievement. Anybody can do this trick!

Rhyme Notes

Rhythm

In a volume of research titled *Rhythm in Psychological, Linguistic, and Musical Processes,* one of the authors found that "the most ubiquitous feature of nature is rhythm." He added, "Understanding rhythm may be the key to understanding the human perceptual process."

Charles A. Elliott also asserted:

"The human mind assumes that a rhythmic principle operates in the whole of man's environment," and that "Language development and comprehension may have a rhythmic basis."

We certainly know that in America, the foundations of written and oral language are based in rhythms. A mother's lullabies and nursery rhymes are frequent first forms of language for newborns. And when children are ready to learn the written language, it begins with the rhythmic beat applied to the alphabet – their ABCs.

The scientists argue that rhythm's power to influence language development lies in the fact that, like rhymes, it can be predicted or anticipated.

They also suggest that "metrical organization makes it easier to remember verbal material. Accent, duration, and temporal spacing affect long and short-term memory." Thus, "rhythmic organization is an important factor in acquiring an important human skill, reading."

They add further that, "Rhythm and number are essentially the same and the entire universe is arranged according to number, that is, rhythm."

Rhythm

Using rhythm, in its various forms, to instruct children in reading and other subjects, can bring about a transformative effect – psychologically, emotionally, and socially.

Education Consultant Harry Wong argues that research has shown that "the number one problem in the classroom is not discipline; it's the lack of procedures and routines. Procedures and routines equal structure…Students risk failure because of lack of structure…"

In The Happy Teacher/Happy Students training, rhythm is employed to establish classroom order and structure (through clapping, instrument ringing or beating, singing, and citing rules to rhymes), to increase vocabulary and comprehension through choral reading, imprinting, and (scaffolded) round-robin reading, as well as in the reading of plays and poetry.

Rhythm also is helpful in devising systems that aid memory of important facts and/or historical events. Rhythm also can be highly effective for stress and trauma relief.

Adding rhythm to learning experiences makes the experience multi-sensory, which enhances excitement and boosts retention. Rhythm helped Helen Keller learn to hear and develop language. It helped the son of Napoleon Hill, who was born with no ears, learn to speak and hear.

The 2007 Benjamin Franklin Silver Book Award Winner *Three Rs Before Reading: Rhythm, Rhyme and Repetition* by Educator and Author Patricia Derrick tells us that "these three Rs fire neurons in the brain. As neurons fire, they make connections. The more stimulating the environment, the more connections made between neurons."

Rhythm Notes

Repetition

"While Western listeners might find repetition boring, non-Western musicians find that repetition helps build intensity..." – Man's Earliest Music by Richard Carlin

According to the National Institute for Literacy's *Reading First* report, issued in 2003, "Repeated and monitored oral reading improves word recognition, speed, accuracy, and fluency and overall reading achievement...To a lesser but still considerable extent, repeated reading also improves comprehension."

When comprehension increases, overall reading ability increases. Not to mention the joy in reading for the reader.

Scientists have found that repetition is an activity that can re-wire the brain and strengthen neurons to enhance learning.

The institute urges that: "Students should read and reread until a certain level of fluency is reached...usually four times is sufficient."

Facts, figures, character backgrounds and characteristics are often repeated in stories so that the reader will keep them high in mind, stay tuned to the story, and happily follow it. With reading repetition, the reader is hearing the words, seeing the words, and saying the words over and over. It's inevitable that something is going to stick.

Consider this perspective from a rap musicologist about looping (playing a break or beat over and over again). "...looping automatically recasts any musical element it touches...After a few repetitions...it begins to gather a compositional weight that far exceeds its original significance..." - Joe Schloss, *Making Beats: The Art of Sample-Based Hip-Hop*

In Partnering for Fluency, Mary Kay Moskal and Camille Blachowicz write that repetition or repeated reading is "decidedly one of the best strategies for fluency development."

The authors also found that repetition provides teachers with <u>*a critical assessment tool*</u> of a student's reading ability and challenges. It provides both teacher and student with instant feedback, and a foundation from which to build greater reading improvement. This is another example of a deliberate system, which, you will recall from our introduction, greatly increases the chances for success.

Repetition

Recall what the scientists said in the early portion of our program: Success is a matter of repetition, guidance, and goal-setting. Repetition might be boring to some, but for the struggling reader, it builds intensity, which translates into fluency, comprehension, and confidence. It can and *should* be used to increase the retention of facts, figures, concepts, words, and events in any subject area.

A case in point:

In 2004, I tutored an Indiana boy named Ivory. Ivory had just finished 5th grade. His teacher said he read on less than a 2nd grade level. He had no fluency and couldn't pronounce a long list of monosyllabic words. He understood and remembered very little of what he read.

I worked with Ivory once a week for about 90 minutes. Before beginning a book with this charming young man, I would ask him to read the book or a chapter to me. I would time him. I would next read the entire book or chapter to Ivory and ask him to follow along as I read. The third time through, I would read a page or a paragraph to Ivory, then ask him to "echo" or repeat what I had read. The fourth and final time through, Ivory would read the entire book or chapter on his own.

Repeatedly, Ivory would at least double his reading speed by the final read-through. For instance, it took him 45 minutes the first time to read *Kara Finds Sunshine on a Rainy Day*. At the end our session, Ivory read *Kara* in less than 20 minutes. After that fourth read, I would ask him questions about the story or chapter to gauge how much he comprehended. He demonstrated that he had a much deeper understanding of what the story was about by the fourth time than he had the first time. As a result, his confidence grew. I could see Ivory's shoulders rise and his face loosen. He would smile in between paragraphs and glance at me to confirm that he was on the right track.

I taped each chapter as I read it and left the tape with Ivory to listen and read to during the week. It made a huge difference. Ivory began to see that the strategy of repetition was making his reading sound fluent for the first time in his life. As soon as I arrived, he would announce to me how much he had read during the past week, instead of waiting for me to inquire. Ivory was eager to begin reading each time we got together and smiled as he more easily breezed through each page of text.

In just three months, he rose about three grade levels.

Repetition Notes

Rap

What...is...funny, sexy, political, heretical, criminal-minded, socially-relevant, child-like, gritty, gory, erotic, psychotic, robotic, ridiculous, conspicuous, angry, lazy, hazy, as powerful as a neutron bomb, antisocial, revolutionary, thievish, thuggish, beautiful, glamorous, awe-inspiring, artistic, sadistic, simplistic, realistic, misogynistic, poetic, a cultural aesthetic, violent, virulent, ambidextrous, materialistic, schiz-o-phren-ic, impoverished, embellished, full of jealousy, misery, envy that you can see, backstabbing, cynical, sarcastic, nostalgic, irreverent, but relevant, some white men's playground, some black men's railroad to freedom, up from the underground, a hit in cities, a smash in the suburbs, bumping through the speakers of the young and hip in every town, across the continent, and over the seas, goes waaaay back before James Brown and Please, Please, Please, Please, before Signifyin' Monkey made you laugh and hit your knees?

Rap is all that and a bag of hope. Today's and yesterday's young people know it. If you want to connect with your students and open your classroom to unbounded creativity, reading and subject mastery, you must not, cannot, dare not, be afraid of rap. Rap is simply the embodiment of rhythm, rhyme and repetition – three highly effective tools in teaching children to become better readers.

So many challenged readers and writers lack the means to express how they feel about what's going on in their lives – whether at home or in school. They don't have the vocabulary. They don't have the confidence. Many times, they are not given the opportunity.

Rap is a tool for self-expression. Anybody can use it, but look at who uses it most – those with the fewest legitimate means of giving their opinions on personal, local, state, national, or international affairs. If they had an empowering way of using their voices in a classroom setting, how much more engaged in the learning experience would they become?

A psychologist speaking on a radio show observed that violence is often the result of a communication breakdown or a lack of communication skills by one party. She was explaining the phenomenon of men beating their wives, especially after women announced that they wanted to leave. But it doesn't take a lot of reflection to see the violent results of communication breakdowns in our everyday lives and in conflicts between and among individuals, organizations, businesses, and political entities.

See page 47 to learn more about Teacher Marni Barron's 2nd Grade reading revolution using rap in Barack Obama: A Hip Hop Tale

Rap

I needed to teach to D.C. Special Education students the difference between nouns and pronouns to meet a 6th grade Language Arts standard. Many of the children were unruly; they regularly cursed blue streaks, constantly made jokes about each other, and talked loudly and out of turn. They all were also three to four grade levels behind in reading and writing.

Slick Rick's *Children's Story* is one of my favorite raps of all time. It has an incredibly infectious beat and it skillfully and humorously reveals an important moral, although there is no happy ending to the song. I also found that *Children's Story* is jam-packed with nouns and pronouns.

I decided to create a rap about the difference between nouns and pronouns and teach it to the students. Next, they would read *Children's Story* to identify nouns and pronouns. The last part of the assignment was for students to write their own story, mixing up the use of nouns and pronouns.

This is the pronoun rap I taught the students:

"A noun is a person, place, or thing, like teacher, city, street, or a diamond ring.
Pronouns take the place of a noun, like she or he sitting in for a clown.
A pronoun by itself doesn't tell you a thing. 'It' could be a car, a house, or a diamond ring."

The teacher and I rapped it. Immediately some of the boys started beating the rhythm on their desks. Others were delighted when I passed out home-made shakers for them to intensify the rhythm. In fact, they enjoyed themselves so much, they didn't want to stop. The teacher and I kept going over the rap, then asked the students to repeat it. We followed up by asking them to give us examples of nouns and pronouns. They were right every time. In a matter of minutes, with rap, we had a cooperative, energized, and engaged classroom of students that many people would have concluded could not be taught.

Below is an excerpt from a rap that begins in *Darius Daniels: Game On*! and got extended with audiences. I was told that a 7-year-old in a recent audience literally couldn't sit still for five minutes. Well, he sat through our entire 90-minute presentation, full of raps and rhymes, transfixed. I've found that children are willing authors or co-authors of a raps on any subject. Use online rhyming dictionaries for assistance, and enjoy!

I love books like kids love candy.
I love books like beaches love sandy.
I love books like corn loves to pop.
I love books like hip loves to hop.
I love books like icing loves cake.
I love books like pies love to bake.
I love books like cars love to drive.
I love books like bees love the hive.

Rap Notes

Routines

Struggling Not to Die

by Caroline Brewer © 2006

Because my mouth is wide and yellin',
and my balled fists scream that I'm rebellin',
And my throat vomits words that attack,
You might not notice that I'm in pain
because I'm poor, feel dumb, and suffer from lack.
Because my mouth is wide and yellin',
and I fight everything in my path,
You might not see the effects of the abuse I'm quellin'.
You might not notice the violence that's been heaped on me.
You might not consider its aftermath.
Because my mouth is wide and yellin',
You might not hear my soul's desperate cry.
Because my feet are kicking people, places, and things,
You might not see me struggling so hard <u>not</u> to die.

Inspired by Minstrel Man by Langston Hughes

In 2007, *Health Day News* reported that children who lost a parent during the September 11 World Trade Center attacks were 10 times as likely to suffer from PTSD as non-bereaved children.

So it's easy to imagine that many of the children attending our schools who have lost a parent, and, in some cases, have lost two parents, are also distressed and suffering from trauma. In more recent times, we have children coming to school after losing parents or other family members to Covid-19.

However, because their losses occur rather silently, in comparison to an international incident such as a terrorist attack, their emotional pain often doesn't register in our assessments of how to educate them.

According to Webster, trauma is "an injury, wound, or shock to the body or mind that produces emotional pain, lasting psychic effects, or a neurosis." A neurosis is a mental disorder which causes psychological pain or discomfort that could be disabling.

From the loud yelling, physical, verbal, and sexual abuse, instability, and disruptions some children receive from their home environments, to the frustrations unleashed by overwhelmed teachers in the classroom, many of today's children attend school in a traumatized state, Joshua Smith says. Often they create drama as a result of it.

Routines

Their behavior can be impulsive, irritable, and hyperactive, as they desperately seek a way to address the mental and emotional pain they are experiencing.

Trauma Researcher Francine Shapiro writes, "When a traumatic or very negative event occurs, information processing may be incomplete."

Let's pause here and consider a few examples, such as how you felt about going to work, cleaning the house, running an errand, or studying for an assignment after the loss of a loved one, or having a partner break up with you, being evicted, having your car repossessed, your child being rushed to the hospital or any number of traumatic experiences. Now think of a child going through similar experiences.

In severe cases, as noted by Harvard Neurologist and Trauma Researcher Bessel Van der Kolk, a person can experience a level of disturbance so severe that it renders him unable to function in everyday activities and inhibits his ability to learn.

As we explained earlier, research shows that the No. 1 reason children fail in school is because of a lack of structure. Classroom routines provide that much-needed structure.

"Words have power...There is life in the words we speak. There is death in the words we speak. There is healing in the words we speak...When you speak to a child, try to take your words off the distress, and center them on something uplifting, something that will quicken a student rather than weaken him."

In addition to routines for structure, this training advocates routines for every aspect of the educational experience, including, and especially, for classroom management. How we routinely speak to children, as discussed in the Relationships chapter, is key to classroom management.

CARPE DIEM (Calm Advantage and Rapport, Pattern Equilibrium, Discharge Interfering Emotions with Mediation) is the Routine developed by Joshua Smith that we recommend to help children who exhibit troublesome behavior and struggle to achieve because of it.

Scientifically, Smith says, the practice of all **CARPE DIEM** elements is known as positive feedback loops, versus the normally and frequently practiced negative feedback loops. These loops are part of an intelligence feedback system between the brain and the endocrine glands to regulate chemical emissions of hormones and neuro-chemicals in the body.

Basically, the brain becomes more excited with positive feedback and more inhibited with negative feedback. Developing a routine of offering positive feedback gives teachers the best chance to get a child to open up and to stop troublesome behavior.

Routines

CARPE DIEM * THE SUPREME 4-STEP ROUTINE

STEP 1: CALM ADVANTAGE: This is the first stage of the **CARPE DIEM ROUTINE**, <u>Calm Advantage</u>. We must remain in control of our emotions every moment we're in contact with children. The easiest way to do this is to be aware that surprising and shocking things will happen, and that we should not take it personally. Children are most likely exhibiting troubling behavior because they're searching for a way to communicate pain, confusion, or stress. Joshua stresses that we remember always to breathe and take the high ground of calm.

STEP 2. RAPPORT: Joshua explains that building <u>Rapport</u> with children happens when we identify with their situation and show empathy, which will give students permission – and a safe and secure opportunity – to explain why they're behaving in a destructive, defeating, or disruptive manner. This is the perfect time to use the Relationship-building phrases, such as "How do you feel?" and "How can I help you?" Refer to the feelings wall and know that in this step you are to do as Stephen R. Covey advocates and "Seek first to understand."

STEP 3. PATTERN EQUILIBRIUM: If the child doesn't want to explain what's wrong, or once she does, give the child an option to do something different than what might have triggered the outburst or misbehavior. This can bring about **Pattern Equilibrium** and balance in the child's emotional state. In other words, intentionally interrupt children's thought patterns by offering a wide-open space for them to play in. It could include writing, drawing, reading, taking a walk, breathing, or other exercises Joshua supplies in the next chapter. You will be amazed at the effect it will have on children. It's all about having more options in your hands, more tools.

Years ago, a first grader had a meltdown, cried and begged not to go to an all-school recreational activity. When the teacher used **CARPE DIEM**, the child calmed down, opened up and told her he didn't want to go to the activity because it always happened just before it was time to go home. And he didn't want to go home because he felt he was always a bother to his mother. This might seem unbelievable, but that afternoon, the child confessed his concerns to his mother in the presence of school officials. With **Pattern Equilibrium,** the adults got to the root of the behavior and it came to an end.

STEP 4. DISCHARGE INTERFERING EMOTIONS WITH MEDIATION: In this stage, find a win-win solution. As Covey says, Win-Win is a total philosophy of human interaction. We get what we reward. Ask children for suggestions and offer suggestions. Avoid judgment. Write them on paper and calmly discuss what might work best for the two of you and the current situation. (Positive Feedback Loops.) Also, if necessary, work out a plan with students that will help them stay alert to their emotions and avoid future outbursts. Get them to make a commitment to the plan, such as the promise you made, and if they deviate, pleasantly, with a smile, remind them of their commitment and of how you intend to keep yours. Stay confident no matter the child's response, knowing that they will rise to your expectations.

Routines

Create with your students a *Feelings Wall* that lists vocabulary they can use to express their emotions and communicate, especially during emotionally challenging times. Below are words in alphabetical order to jumpstart your classroom wall. It's structured to answer, "How do you feel?" or "How are you?" Use as many as you like but please leave room for students to contribute more.

The Feelings Wall

afraid, agitated, alert, alive, amused, angry, anxious, apathetic, appreciative, ashamed, awful, bad, beautiful, bitter, blissful, bold, bored, captivated, comfortable, confident, confused, cool, content, creative, dead, delighted, depressed, determined, disappointed, dumb,

elated, elegant, enchanted, energetic, enthralled, enthusiastic, enraged, envious, excited, exhilarated, fancy, fatigued, frail, fraudulent, frugal, good, graceful, gratified, great, gregarious, horrible, hurt, hyped,

icky, impatient, indifferent, insecure, inspired, invigorated, joyful, jubilant, like a champion, like crap, like a queen, like the king of the world, languid, logy, lonely, mad, melancholy, mellow, mindful, miserable, negative, nervous, numb, optimistic, pained, passive, passionate, peaceful, pensive, pleased, puzzled,

quizzical, raw, regretful, relaxed, relieved, rejuvenated, resentful, sad, satisfied, scared, shocked, sick, silly, small, smart, sore, spastic, sunny, super-duper, sympathetic,

threatened, tickled, tired, triumphant, uncomfortable, uplifted, victorious, vigorous, warm, weak, wise, witty, wounded, zany

Routines Notes

Release and Relax

In *The Happy Teacher/Happy Students,* Smith recommends eye movements, breathing exercises, and powerful body expressions to bilaterally stimulate the brain while positively interrupting the effects of trauma and creating more peaceful and positive messages. These exercises allow the child to relax, adapt to new information, and enjoy being a child, as well as enjoy the learning experience.

Most of our energy and information is recorded through our eyes, according to Smith. The optic nerve runs through both hemispheres of the brain, and when we see something disturbing, we are easily aroused if there is a previously disturbing memory that involved visual input.

When children grow up in continuously oppressive circumstances, this translates into continuous arousal and hyper-vigilance. Smith says children are slowly conditioned to believe something "bad" will happen, because they have seen and bi-laterally experienced so many "bad" things. When children are in a hyper-vigilant state, they are less likely to draw distinctions between healthy and unhealthy situations.

This certainly was the case in the Gulf Coast, where children who lived through Hurricane Katrina and the flooding by the levees later demonstrated PTSD symptoms. The Children's Health Fund, which is an arm of the National Center for Disaster Preparedness, found that these children began quickly suffering from nightmares, increased anxiety, sadness, and anger, and were more likely to commit violence.

Suicide and depression increased, and many were unable to distinguish between healthy and unhealthy situations.

Consider the elementary student who threatens suicide, murder, and has outbursts so violent, school staff feel compelled to restrain him. Is there another way to reach children like this? Is there another way to teach them? Absolutely.

Traumatized children need opportunities to discharge their "frozen" or stuck reactions. It can begin with the relationship building phrases, such as "How do you feel?" or "How can I help you?" followed by the **CARPE DIEM** routine we outlined (Calm Advantage and Rapport, Pattern Equilibrium, Discharge Interfering Emotions with Mediation).

Release and Relax

Clapping Rhythmically: Clapping is one of the most natural and powerful exercises to bilaterally stimulate brain hemispheres. By instructing children to stand up and clap while looking at their palms and listening to the clapping sounds, they will begin to pump themselves up, and activate the visual, auditory and kinesthetic centers in the brain. Increasing the volume of the clapping intensifies the feeling. Adding a sound, such as "ha ha ha ha ha," as the children clap opens them to experiencing greater excitement and concentration. It's a challenge, and that's good news, because children love challenges.

A simple clapping rhythm is to clap three times in even spaces, such as 1,2,3 – 1,2,3 – 1,2,3. You can also try the ubiquitous rhythm 1,2,3 (pause), 4,5. Do each clapping rhythm three or four times and then invite your students to share a beat. Clap to their beat three or four times, and then invite another student to share a beat. Four or five distinct beats from your students should be enough to get rid of any tension or anxiety.

Clapping Rhythmically also helps snap students to attention when they might be distracted, or become too talkative. This eliminates the need for a teacher to raise his voice or pound a desk. It's also good to use before the introduction of a lesson, speaker, or practice. It can be especially fun and captivating if used as a musical instrument during the reading of a book, story, or poetry. I always use regular hand claps to acknowledge students who participate in classroom discussions or activities. In Ghana, a third grade teacher named Madam Victoria used the 1,2,3 (pause) 4,5 clap to reward participation. Ask your students to create a beat that you can use to reward participation and watch their confidence soar.

The Masaai Bounce: The Masaai Bounce (after the Masaai tribe in Africa) is where children lightly bound up and down while they clap. This stimulates endorphins, oxygenates the blood, and opens up the brain to deeper learning.

Mirror Dancing: Put on fun, danceable music and have the children face each other in pairs. One partner begins a movement and the other partner follows that movement exactly. Children are encouraged to be creative and expressive in leading the movement. Eye contact is important in this exercise. To get the students off to an orderly start, you might start out by doing some movements and ask all the children to mirror them. This can also work in the virtual world, so don't be shy!

Release & Relax Notes

The Rapture, Eye Scissors

The Rapture: Joshua says shaking the entire body – hands, feet, shoulders, hips – builds energy! Begin by introducing the Rapture with a metaphor, such as "Let's go for a ride on the Rapture Train!" Let this wild shaking go on for about 10 seconds, then allow students to shake their heads and open their mouths and make a noise, such as 'Ahhh!' as they let loose. Allow this exercise to go for 30-45 seconds. End the exercise by announcing you are bringing the ride to a close by saying something such as, "We're getting off the Rapture Train at the next stop." Then invite your students to become still and inhale deeply through the nose. Hold the breath, tighten every muscle in the body and then release by exhaling through the mouth. Continue deep inhales and exhales two more times.

Joshua argues **the Rapture** is an excellent way to bring children back to a calm and relaxed place when "rowdiness" appears in a few of the children and the teacher needs to quickly regain a calm advantage. The Rapture is also a great way to reward children for completing an assignment. This exercise works well as a sequel to clapping.

Eye Scissors: Begin with palms facing the body. Lift arms outward in front of the body, and hold the palms at the level of the chin. Bend the elbows so that the palms are now just a foot or so away from the face. Begin quickly folding the arms inward toward the midline of the body keeping the 12-inch distance between the arms and the front of the body. Pay attention to the left hand and forearm, making sure that they are closest to the front of the body. Allow the palms to cross each other to form an "X," then separate the arms by bringing them outward to the original start position. Repeat.

When repeating, allow the opposite arm or right arm and hand to fall inward, closest to the front of the body. This leaves the left hand and arm outside. Have the children forcefully say, "I want more brain power!" over and over. The louder they are, the more exciting it is for them, and the deeper the message sinks into their unconscious to be open to learning.

Another great tool to enhance **CARPE DIEM** is the use of **treadmills**. If your school had one on site, imagine that when a child got heated and ready to act out, she'd be escorted to a room with the treadmill. She'd be invited to take a walk or run on the treadmill for a few minutes to regain her equilibrium through exercising and breathing. Joshua reveals that the experience of walking and breathing is sometimes enough to stimulate both halves of the brain and allow children to relax.

Walks, Fountains & Peace Gardens

Have you ever gone out for a walk or a jog after a stressful day and felt 100 times better afterwards? Why not teach children this valuable lesson? How empowering for students to learn to be more responsible for their emotional state and to learn to be proactive. In an elementary school in D.C. where fights broke out routinely, students who had been taught to breathe deeply began the practice of taking deep breaths when they felt stressed or angry and the staff told us the practice led to fewer physical confrontations.

To reiterate, children act out because they are attempting to discharge interfering emotions. Their bodies are low in serotonin and Joshua says that they don't have the skills to modulate a peaceful response when they suddenly are overwhelmed with adrenalin and endorphins. Getting them to consciously take care of their emotional imbalance is another rapport building experience. Think of the time when you yourself were completely stressed out and found a way to get on a treadmill, take a jog, or do some other type of physical activity. You clearly had other – less positive – options available to you. But if you chose to release your tension through exercise, your body and mind surely thanked you for it.

We understand that most schools, especially at the elementary, middle and junior high levels, don't have treadmills. But think of how many people, organizations, and gyms in your community have excess amounts of exercise equipment. If you notify them of your need, we are willing to bet that someone will respond by donating one or more.

Another option: Consider having the principal, counselor or security guard take the student for a walk outside or around the building. Consider, also, a water feature in the classroom, such as a **small fountain**, or creating **a garden** on school grounds – and give it a special name – where children can go to relax and find release. Make sure you have signs indicating why the garden and fountain are there.

Inviting students to write or draw, or in some way illustrate, are other incredibly powerful tools for releasing tension and discharging interfering emotions. If a child wants to put his head down or take a nap to cope with emotional stress or pain, please be open to such an option until you can create a plan that allows him to release tension and stay engaged in learning.

Release & Relax Notes

Relevance

Relevance - Pertaining to the matter at hand, to the point, close logical relationship, applicable; inspires revolutions

One of the most effective ways to bring relevance into the classroom and boost children's literacy skills is to invite children to write essays, letters, poems, short stories, and "books" about books they've read, or experiences during holidays, weekends, vacations, or even ordinary events, such as a school rule.

I've witnessed small miracles working with D.C. high school students, up to six grade levels behind in reading, who wrote essays for a class book on the subject *What You Don't Know by Looking at Me.*

I worked with 400 elementary students in Prince George's County to write thank you cards and letters to President Barack and First Lady Michelle Obama during their final months in office (because expressing gratitude is an important part of personal growth, right?). President Obama wrote a letter back to the children (how meaningful was that!) and all of the correspondence is in a book on Amazon called *For the Obamas: A Big Book of Thank Yous.* Most of the children had never written thank you letters or used computers to compose writing. It took months and many drafts, but afterwards, every student was more at ease with writing and self-expression.

Below are excerpts from some of the student's letters:

Dear Mr. President and Mrs. Obama,

Thank you for everything you did for America. You have a nice picture in our classroom. We hope you come back some day. We will protect the city until you come back.
– Love, Ms. Turner's Kindergarten Class

You guys have been helpful to people all across the world. You helped people who were sick and you've helped people get jobs. You guys have saved lives and made health care more available to citizens and more affordable. Thank you, again, for your service.
– Most respectfully, Travis, 5th Grade

Thank you for keeping our homes safe. Thank you for being nice and for making the world helpful. We will miss you.
– Love, Ms. Reilly's First Grade Class

We hope that you have great last days in the White House. We are glad you have been our president and First Lady for 8 years. We hope you will be safe and happy. President and Mrs. Obama, I thank you for talking to kids in a nice way. I hope you will have a nice future.
– Most respectfully, Matthew, 3rd Grade

Relevance

I also used relevance for the lessons I taught the Special Education middle-schoolers. For instance, we started out reading *Kara Finds Sunshine*. It's a picture book, and typically would be below the reading level of 6th and 7th graders. However, to keep the students from feeling that the book would be relevant only to "little kids," I gave the history of the book (this edition was dedicated to Hurricane Katrina survivors) and engaged them in a discussion and review of facts about the storm and flood.

Two weeks after first reading the book, I traveled to New Orleans and returned with pictures and stories about what I saw. I compared the survivors' conditions to the conditions in the city where we all lived – Washington, D.C. I next invited students to write a letter to Katrina survivors based on our discussion. These students were not in the habit of beginning, much less, completing, any writing assignment. They had little faith in their abilities. And yet, some of the most thoughtful sentiments I've ever seen adolescents express came from that assignment.

Here are some *unedited* examples:

"I am sorry about the people died in the Katrina and I like the people survived the Katrina and I wish I can bring money and food to the kids…" (in the left-hand corner, he draws a small male figure with "I Love You" beneath it.)

"Im in the 7th grade. I sorry for what happen to you. I feel very sad that some of you lost your home and your family and your friends. And I hope you can see the sun again. And I will pray to God for you every day and night…"

"Dear Katrina survivor: Can you tell me how you survive the herricane? Where did you hide at? What did you eat? How did it look? Was it scary?...Did you lose some friends? Did you lose some family or a cousin? Were you sad? Sorry for how you lose so much and who you miss…"

Writing short "books" and illustrating them was a lesson in relevance that changed the reading fortunes of a 4th grader I tutored over six months. Elizabeth had been declared "borderline mentally retarded" and could not read a sentence. I read new picture books to her each week. Her mother continued reading each selection in between our sessions. When we got together again, I encouraged Elizabeth to write her own version of the story – she could change names and add details, such as a hairstyle, clothing, colors, and location. Elizabeth felt empowered. In one week, she was reading and recognizing words she couldn't recognize the week before. Her vocabulary and fluency grew. She also became happier as we read and made new "books."

Six months after we began working together, Elizabeth had authored more than a dozen books and graduated to reading longer and more complex works. Early into her 5th grade year, Elizabeth's mom emailed me to say that she was having her "best school year ever," and Elizabeth wrote, "I love you. I like to read."

Mission joyfully accomplished!

Relevance

When I traveled to Ghana to create an alphabet book, the teachers and I led the students on a field trip through Konko Village to identify fruits, vegetables, plants, and flowers for the book we were creating. A village boy joined us as we walked the roads and ran ahead to point out a garden egg. It looks like a small cucumber but tastes like squash. Although he wasn't in our class, in no time at all, he found what we were teaching relevant enough to become engaged and contribute to our book!

Ron Clark, former Disney Teacher of the Year, explained: "We did worksheets that taught them how to keep score before we went to bowl…We plotted our course on maps and estimated the amount of fuel we would need…We learned about sea creatures and erosion before heading to the beach…All the students get excited because the work has something to do with going on a trip…Not only do they retain information at a faster rate, but they also want to learn because they see it as relevant. Something they'll be using and experiencing in the near future…"

Clark's examples demonstrate that when a lesson in school can be applied to real life, students become excited and that makes teaching and learning more rewarding.

"The interview" is the primary and brilliant way that Paula Rogovin for years taught her New York City students every subject they need to learn during the school year. "The interview" brings authors, artists, musicians, parents, grandparents, sculptors, and all sorts of folks into the classroom to be grilled, politely, by the first graders, about what they do and how they do it. Through the interviews, which are conducted also at the workplaces, the children learn math, history, science, and literacy.

After questioning guests for 30 minutes, and recording the information in notebooks, the tykes make "books" that summarize what they learned. They draw pictures and write poems and prose based on what they heard and observed. Ultimately, they learn a lot more than what anyone would ever think to put on a test. And speaking of tests, Rogovin's students at Manhattan New School P.S. 290 average 90 percent on achievement tests.

Lastly, this poem writing exercise changed all of my students, but this third grader experienced a real revolution from anger at the world to self-love and harmony after being given this assignment and being supported through her emotional outbursts to complete it.

I feel love for myself when I dance.
I feel love for myself when I dance because it makes me feel happy
and also helps me get all my anger out.

I feel love when I am riding my hover board.
I feel love for myself when
I'm riding my hover board because I feel powerful.

I feel love for myself when I'm doing the splits.
I feel love for myself when I'm doing the splits because I feel talented.
It feels powerful to love myself.

Relevance Notes

Recreation

Recreation - Refreshment in Body and Mind; Having fun.

"Children today have little difficulty telling us when they feel bored. Often they state it indignantly and with blameful gusto...When we look at the causes of boredom, we begin to see why (work and learning) are two fields of endeavor that are fertile ground for its occurrence...Monotony...and constraint contribute to boredom." – Raymond J. Wlodkowski and Judith H. Jaynes, authors of *Eager to Learn*

In *Two Parts Textbook, One Part Love*, renowned teacher and author LouAnne Johnson has this to say about making school work more fun – during test time, no less. "Laughter reduces tension...You can inspire smiles by personalizing your exams. Replace city names with local neighborhoods, and business names with local stores. If a school is mentioned, change its name to that of your school. If you create your own exams, include your students' names in the questions." This also, of course, is a case of making matters relevant. It's the tactic I used with a Special Education 4th grader that changed her life.

As Johnson puts it, "No matter how old they act, children are still children, and they need to laugh, to play, to create, to stretch their imaginations, and tickle their brains... Laughter heals the body, soothes the soul, and stimulates the brain. It also makes a long school day much more enjoyable."

That goes for both educators and students. Vocabulary "BINGO" is one of my favorite recreational educational tools. It was also a big hit with Special Education middle-schoolers who said they wanted to *play* more than learn academics. So I created vocabulary "BINGO" cards based on rhyming words, proper nouns, historical figures and places, and themes from reading materials we used. We gave quarters and Reese's Cups to the winning students.

A boy who had started the school year with an unbelievably foul mouth but had calmed down in recent weeks (because of our relationship strategies), won the most "BINGO" games and was going home with $1.75 and three Reese's Cups. He sat quietly, looked up, and then as a wide grin spread across his face, solemnly declared, "This is the happiest day of my life."

Recreation, as you see, is not just about playing, although in a school setting, playing ought to be allowed and encouraged. Recreation, indeed, is also about healing. If our students and we teachers need anything, we need healing. It is my fervent hope that every component of the Happy Teacher/Happy Students strategy leads to exactly that.

*See instructions on page 49 for how to create Vocabulary "BINGO" cards for your students.

Recreation Notes

General Notes

Background

President Obama's historic journey to the White House inspires 2nd graders to win at reading

WASHINGTON, D.C. - June 4, 2009 – "Books can change lives." That is the mantra of the Children's Book Council (CBC), which designates a week each year to celebrate books for young readers.

In a D.C.-area classroom, that mantra was in daily practice. Through her creative use of a new children's book to teach every Language Arts standard, a teacher turned a class of second graders – many of whom read below grade level – into enthusiastic, confident, and higher achieving readers.

The book, *Barack Obama: A Hip Hop Tale of King's Dream Come True*, is a humorous, satirized and fictionalized account of the presidential campaign written by Author and Education consultant Caroline Brewer of Washington, D.C. The book's swift-moving rhymes, rhythm and drama entertain while educating children about one of the most important events in world history. The brightly illustrated 32-page book ultimately reveals President Obama's powerful connection to the enduring legacy of the Rev. Dr. Martin Luther King, Jr. and the Civil Rights Movement Dr. King so courageously led.

"I have been amazed at what this book has done not only to teach my second-graders about President Obama's historic journey to the White House, but also at how it has taught my children to become much better readers," says Marni Barron, who teaches at Dodge Park Elementary in Landover, Md. "Never before have I had all class members want to read so desperately, and ultimately, improve in reading so quickly!"

"One student, who was disruptive and usually tuned out of learning, suddenly tuned in. Because I allowed the students to stand and tap to the rhythm of the text, he began to think of reading time as fun-time," says Barron, who has taught for 15 years and is a former reading coach. "Some of my best days teaching have (involved) using this book."

And clearly with the results these second graders have seen, some of their best days learning to read have come with *Barack Obama: A Hip Hop Tale* and reading improvement strategies by Brewer.

When Ms. Barron first began teaching these students on January 5, 2009, only four of her 14 students were reading on grade level, according to their December Scholastic Reading Inventory (SRI) evaluations. By late March, all of the students were reading at or above grade level on two assessments, the DRA (Developmental Reading Assessment) and Leveled Readers. Eight students were on grade level according to the SRI and six were still below, although most of those students had gains ranging from 100 to 400 points.

Background

The Happy Teacher reading strategies encourage a holistic approach to reading instruction that focuses on building good relationships with students, positive reinforcement, the use of relevant materials and entertaining techniques, such as rhythm, rhyme, and rap.

"This book, Ms. Brewer's Happy Teacher reading strategies, and our new president are responsible for some amazing achievement gains," said Ms. Barron. "The student who had been a behavior problem no longer causes trouble now that he reads on grade level. (Another) student, who, until late February, was still learning the sounds of the alphabet, is now reading books above grade level."

Brewer says *Barack Obama: A Hip Hop Tale of King's Dream Come True* was written to support the reading strategies designed to give teachers – especially those in low-resource schools – a powerful and entertaining educational resource.

Cheryl Thomas, Ed.D., agrees that Brewer's work has strong, positive implications for children and teachers across the country. "(With) the (Happy Teacher), Brewer provides practical strategies to help struggling readers succeed, not only with reading and writing, but with independent learning skills. Brewer's (work) calls for renewed focus on teaching that can reap rewards for students and instructors. (The Happy Teacher) is a must for educators intent on improving instruction, reaching the seemingly disconnected student, and creating magic within the classroom."

Olatokunbo (Toks) S. Fashola, Ph.D., a Maryland-based senior research fellow at Optimal Solutions Group, an adjunct research scientist and faculty associate at Johns Hopkins University, has conducted research and published books and articles on the effectiveness of comprehensive school reform programs as well as reading intervention programs. Fashola believes the progress achieved by Barron's students is significant and a good candidate for scientific study.

Brewer looks forward to seeing her work and the experience of Barron and her students explored and evaluated by more educational institutions, their teachers and students. "The need for reading materials and strategies that are holistic and engaging, and that help boost language skills could not be more urgent. I believe that what has happened in Ms. Barron's classroom can happen in any classroom. I look forward to seeing more children experience the tremendous joy of being great readers and highly motivated learners."

Ask Caroline for details on how to recreate this lesson!

Creating Vocabulary "BINGO" Cards

Obama	mama	kid	bid	cope
hope	frogs	dogs	hogs	sent
president	go		care	everywhere
sent	know	sun	agreed	proceed
creed	sow	run	day	say

Barack Obama: A Hip Hop Tale Vocabulary Rhyming Cards ©2008

Begin with a list of at least 30 words. On an 8.5 x 11 sheet of blank paper, draw 25 squares, including a Free Space in the center, or use the blank Vocabulary BINGO card on the next page.

Each word from your vocabulary list should be written on separate index cards or small squares of paper and those cards should be placed in a container.

Players should review the list to find the 24 words they want to write on their game cards.

After game cards are made, begin the game by drawing the index cards from the container and announcing them one at a time.

Give players a chance to locate the term on their cards. Use plastic chips, pennies, M&Ms®, or small paper squares as chips.

A winning card will have five items in a row - across, down, or diagonally - (including free space) covered. The winner should announce, "I got Vocabulary BINGO!"

Play until you're satisfied.

Happy Teacher and Happy Students Training Manual   *Caroline Brewer*

Vocabulary "BINGO" Card

Happy Teacher and Happy Students Training Manual   *Caroline Brewer*

60 Sets of "BINGO" Rhyming Words

From Barack Obama: A Hip Hop Tale of King's Dream Come True

1) street, meet, feet
2) hope, cope, dope
3) basketball, hall
4) sent, president
5) kid, did, bid
6) see, tree, be
7) agreed, proceed
8) eyes, realize
9) understand, land
10) say, day
11) fear, dear
12) skin, within
13) frogs, dogs, hogs
14) know, go
15) being, seeing
16) lose, moves
17) sure, endure
18) voice, choice
19) care, everywhere
20) sun, run
21) frown, down, drown
22) creed, indeed
23) dumb, from
24) side, pride
25) friend, end
26) box, knocks, socks
27) depressed, quest
28) quick, St. Nick
29) hit, quit
30) sneered, cheered
31) Obama, mama
32) hurray, away
33) flap, nap
34) night, uptight
35) soon, moon
36) ear, near
37) air, fair
38) danger, stranger
39) good, neighborhood
40) time, slime
41) rise, skies
42) sure, endure
43) net, bet
44) alive, jive
45) will, kill
46) tall, fall
47) came, same
48) there, mayor
49) places, faces
50) blue, too
51) sow, ago
52) loud, proud
53) white, right, fright
54) too, anew
55) right, sight
56) win, grin
57) school, rule
58) skin, begin
59) you, through
60) around, sound

Happy Teacher and Happy Students Training Manual   *Caroline Brewer*

48 Vocabulary "BINGO" Words

From *Barack Obama: A Hip Hop Tale of King's Dream Come True*

1) bamboozled
2) bare-fanged
3) basketball
4) blossom
5) bores
6) burden
7) campaign
8) cancel
9) charity
10) citizens
11) citizens
12) Colorado
13) commercials
14) courageous
15) deserve
16) division
17) doubters
18) endured
19) energized
20) fired up
21) gravely
22) grouchy
23) guiding
24) honor
25) humanizing
26) lame
27) Malia & Sasha
28) mayor
29) Michelle
30) mocked
31) Nevada
32) Niagara Falls
33) opposition
34) parents
35) presidential
36) rejoiced
37) revolutionary
38) saluted
39) soap opera
40) spreading
41) struggles
42) unity
43) unrepentant
44) verbal
45) violence
46) voices
47) wages
48) wasteland

Happy Teacher and Happy Students Training Manual — *Caroline Brewer*

Bibliography

Adler, Bill. *Rap: Portraits and Lyrics of a Generation of Black Rockers.*

Allen, Jeffrey S. and Klein, Roger J. 1996. *Ready, Set, R.E.L.A.X.* Watertown, WI. Inner Coaching.

Beergamini, Andrea. 1999. *Masters of Music: Music of the World* Barrons Educational Series, Inc.

Breaux, Annette. 2003. *101 Answers for New Teachers and Their Mentors.* Eye on Education. Larchmont, NY.

Carlin, Richard. 1987. *The World of Music: Man's Earliest Music.* Facts on File Publications.

Cherry, Clare. 1983. *Please Don't Sit on the Kids.* Fearon Teacher Aids. Carthage, Illinois.

Clark, Ron. *The Essential Raps.* 2003. Hyperion. New York.

Clark, Ron. The Essential 55, 2003. Hyperion. New York.

Clark, Ron. *The Excellent 11.* 2004. Hyperion. New York.

Cooper, Michael L. 2001. *Slave Spirituals and The Jubilee Singers.* Clarion Books. New York.

Derrick, Patricia. 2006. *The Three Rs Before Reading: Rhythm, Rhyme, and Repetition.*

Dietz, Betty Warner and Olaturnji, Michael Babatunde. 1965. *Musical Instruments of Africa: Their Nature, Use, and Place in The Life of a Deeply Musical People.* New York. The John Day Company.

Floyd, Samuel A. 1995. *The Power of Black Music.* Oxford University Press. New York.

Faber, Adele and Mazlish, Elaine.1995. *How to Talk So Kids Can Learn.* Fireside. New York.

Franklin, Benjamin. 1749. *Proposals Relating to the Education of Youth in Pennsylvania.*

Bibliography

George, Nelson. *Hip Hop America.* 1998. New York. The Penguin Group or Penguin Putnam.

Hughes, Langston. *The Dream Keeper and other Poems* 1994. New York. Alfred A. Knopf.

Hughes, Langston. 1955, 1976, 1982. *The First Book of Jazz.* Hopewell, N.J. The Ecco Press.

Igus, Toyomi. 1998. *I See Rhythm.* San Francisco, CA. Children's Book Press.

Johnson, LouAnne. 1998. *Two Parts Textbook, One Part Love.* Hyperion. New York.

Jones, LeRoi. 1963. *Blues People: Negro Music in White America.* New York. Morrow Quill Paperback.

Jones, Maurice K. 1994.*Say It Loud: The Story of Rap Music.* Millbrook Press.

Kafele, Baruti. 2004. *A Handbook for Teachers of African American Children.* Jersey City, N.J. Baruti Publishing. Jersey City.

Kohl, Herb. *The Discipline of Hope.* 1998. New York. Simon & Schuster.

Moskal, Mary K. and Blachowicz, Camille. 2006. *Partnering for Fluency.* The Gilford Press. New York. London.

Mountrose, Phillip. 1997. *Getting Thru to Kids.* Sacramento, CA. Holistic Communications.

Nagel, Greta. 1994. *The Tao of Teaching.* Donald I. Fine, Inc.

Ridenour, Chuck, with Jah, Yusuf. *Fight The Power: Rap, Race, and Reality*. 1997. Delta Paperbacks.

Schloss, Joseph G. 2004. *Making Beats: The Art of Sample-Based Hip-Hop.* Middletown, CT. Wesleyan University Press,

Wlodkowski, Raymond J. and Jaynes, Judith H. Jaynes. 1990. *Eager to Learn.* San Francisco, CA. Jossey-Bass Publishers.

Wong, Harry K and Rosemary T. *The First Days of School.* Mountainview, CA. Harry K. Wong Publications.

About the Authors

Caroline Brewer is an education consultant, literacy activist, former classroom teacher and reading coach, and author of 12 books, She has made presentations to more than 25,000 teachers, students, parents, and librarians in the U.S. and abroad. Her books for adults include *The Happy Teacher/Happy Students, Why I Teach: A Guide to Re-Discovering the Love of Teaching, Parent Power: How to Raise a Reading Superstar, Having Fun Teaching Math,* and the forthcoming *Having Fun Teaching Writing.*

Ms. Brewer's children's books currently available include *Darius Daniels: Game On!, Kara Finds Sunshine on a Rainy Day, The Jelani Tree, Barack Obama: A Hip Hop Tale of King's Dream Come True,* and *Collard Greens and Yams: A Rhythmic, Rhyming Soul Food Odyssey,* a book for all ages.

Ms. Brewer is a member of the National Council of Teachers of English, a veteran in the communications field, having worked in public relations, TV, radio, newspapers, and served on two Pulitzer Prize juries. A collection of her Sunday newspaper columns was nominated for the Pulitzer. The first column was entered into *The Congressional Record*.

Joshua I. Smith is an internationally practicing authority on movement and healing therapies that are underpinned by 20+ years of research that has led to an exceptional understanding of brain and body functions. He is an author of two chapters dealing with stress relief, relaxation, and trauma relief strategies in *The Happy Teacher/Happy Students* by Education Consultant Caroline Brewer.

His contributions to *The Happy Teacher* include powerful stress and behavioral de-escalation techniques, along with exercises that help stimulate the positive emotional and mental reactions that children need to focus on instruction. These techniques also assist teachers, counselors, and social workers in managing the outbursts of emotionally challenged students.

Born and reared in Washington, D.C., Smith has appeared on television in the US and UK including CBS News, ITV, Channel 4, QVC, Living TV, with numerous radio appearances on BBC, London Broadcasting Company, and has presented exercise seminars and classes, as well as corporate training seminars worldwide. His *Yogaboxing* DVD was the No. 1 selling non-celebrity fitness title in the UK for the 2002/2003 season.

Smith has recently been acknowledged by The Trauma Center and Harvard University's Dr. Bessel van der Kolk, the leading researchers in the field of Post Traumatic Stress Disorder, for his participation in utilizing yoga to diminish the effects of trauma.

www.ingramcontent.com/pod-product-compliance
Lightning Source LLC
Chambersburg PA
CBHW080416170426
43194CB00015B/2830